Poetry

by

Susie Lynn

<u>Coming Soon</u>

Book 2: Darling, Rise Again

Book 3: Darling, Keep Rising

Book 4: Darling, What If?

(See All "Rise" Series coming in 2022:
Instagram @soulful.susie)

Darling, Rise

Uplifting, Juicy, Poetic Morsels

By

Susie Lynn

There are Affirmations.

There are Mantras.

AND THERE ARE …

DARLING UPLIFTERS

For any human needing a pick-me-up.

Lovely, Funny, Sweet, Quirky.

Enjoy!

Darling,

When are you going to
Stop
Pouring out so much &
Start
Pouring in?

Darling,

Get Curious
Not Critical

Be Kind to you
Be Gentle

Darling,

You long to be you
...
Yet you keep fitting in

Darling,

You are here to
Practice Being Human
Not to
Precisely Solve Humanhood

Darling,

Tears intelligently release stress hormones

You are not too sensitive

You are sensate-ly sensational

Darling,

With every deep breath in,
Remember as you exhale,
You're helping a tree survive

Darling,

I know it's hard

But you've done
Hard things before
That turned out
…orgasmically

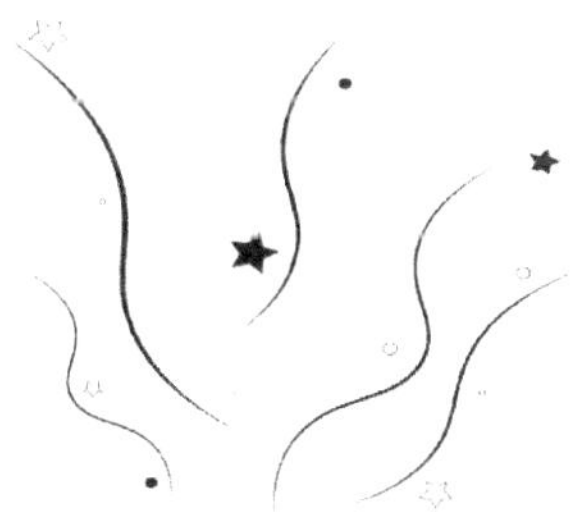

Darling,

Without rest,
your soul hath not
the energy to
come out and play

Darling,

You'll never find what you're
looking for
When you are looking out there

Close your eyes and
Feel Inside

It's there
Tucked sweetly inside of you

Darling,

Real Charm Resides
In a Field of Exquisite Wild
Flowers
Casting Aromatic Spells

Captivating Collisions with
Cosmic Colors
Swirling in
Northern Light Precision

Enchantment Blinking of Fireflies
Synchronous
Luminous
Dancing

Seduction of the Seasonally Ripest
Garnet Jewels of Pomegranate

Darling,

You've done enough today
Sit back and enjoy
Sunset's enchanting hues

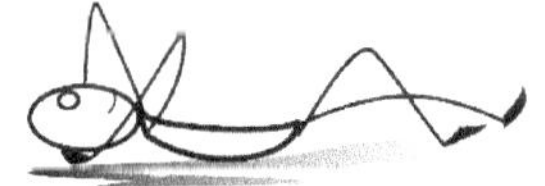

Darling,

If
Variety is the
Spice of Life,

Gratitude is the
Decadent Dessert
of Life

Darling,

The Proof is in
Your Existence

You are Enough

Darling,

May you be as colorful as a
Sunset Moth

As empathetic as an
Elephant

As intelligent as an
Octopus

As curious as a
Cat

--->

As wise as a
Crow

As creative as an
Otter

And as playful as a
Dolphin

Darling,

It's a symbiotic world

Of course
You Matter
More than you know

Darling,

I wish I could let
You see YOU
From my Eyes

Then maybe you'd
See all the Beauty
Your lens
Somehow forgot to
Emphasize

Darling,

Keep your chin up

You never know
When you need to
Look out for bird poo

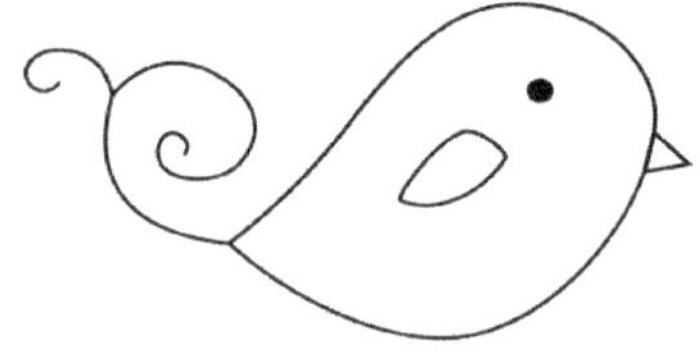

Darling,

If at first
You don't
Succeed

You have
Many more
Options

Darling,

When faced with a not-so-nice
person,

Zig-Zag
Run like wild…
It works for rabbits.

Throw on some grass
Roll in the mud…
Blending works great
for most animals
not to be ate.

Stand taller
Stand larger
Puff out your chest…
Bluffing is the tactic
of cobras and pufferfish.

Be noisy
Use your voice
Rattle
Screech an utmost disaster,
mimicry of another animal…
Advice from a snake,
and a Lyrebird ringmaster.

Or cover your ears…
Deaf moths know how
To cancel noise to
predacious leers,
camo auditory.

Act strange, be colorful,
Confusing the predator
is the name of the game…
says the dragonfly and
perhaps the damsel.

Darling,

Don't stress yourself out.

A stressed octopus eats itself

Darling,

You say you want your partner to
Honor your love language:
Words of Affirmations,

Yet, the way you speak to
Yourself so unkindly…
Do you see how misaligning?

Darling,

If it has been a day of unease,
Put on your jammies,
Escape in a book…

And look,
I don't have all the answers
But if you stir some hot cocoa
And try, And try again when
You're ready to go,

Eventually, you'll be alright
And braver
Figuring out what's in your favor

Darling,

You're trying to capture air!

Pursuit of Happiness
is the most elusive, nonsensical,
soul debauchery

Try Instead:

Pursuit of Purpose

Darling,

You might just be
One toot away
From relief

Darling,

You worry
They are 100%
Positivity Packaged in
Beautiful Ribbons

Don't worry!
If you pull the bow
And look inside the
Delusional package
Of smiley emojis

You will find
Another human being

You will see,
They are not so different inside.

Darling,

You survived a pandemic

Next time you are lonely,
You might be tempted to
Hump the nearest barista bar
when you come out of torpor
In need of a caffeine cure
per se …

But schedule a massage
Or call a
Professional Cuddler instead,
eh?!

Darling,

The merry-go-round
is only stationary
When there's no one
There to push it

Darling,

If you are uncertain

then you'll certainly
be comfortably familiar

when uncertainty
comes calling

Darling,

Your
Body
Is
Begging
To
Be
Loved

Darling,

If you want things to be
Different
You must first
Imagine a
Different way

Darling,

If you think your
Self-doubt is sabotaging

Then I confidently
Think you are right

37

Darling,
Be careful who you
Sleep with

Loud snorers will
Leave you unrested

But snuggly
Cat Cuddles
Will have you waking
Your bestest

Darling,

If you think you are
Too small to be brave

Watch
Honey Badger
Videos

Tiny, but fiercely mighty!
Have courage, they say

Darling,

Wonderful things
Blossom in
Swamplands

No, seriously, though

Darling,

You say you
Want to feel
Better

Yet you keep
Listening and adhering
To that inner voice
That others have been
engineering

Darling,

Feel

    And

        Flow
    &

Flow
    And
        Feel

Darling,

You say you are
Insignificant

But that statement
has zero
value of significance

However, the
You that is You
is Magic
through and through

You were created
Now
Stand Tall

Darling,

If a tiny tardigrade
cutie water bear
could survive an
apocalypse
...
You my dear,
Can make it
Through today

Darling,

Sometimes, Taking the high road
Is just fine, But sometimes …
It means
You're allowing abuse
Sacrificing yourself,
For their amuse.

Assess…
When to Ballerina Pivot,
Walk away

When to Warrior Waltz
Stand firm,
Announce Boundaries Loud
and learn

When to not even engage
And just stay, stay away

Darling,

You can't just keep
Progressively Progressing

Sometimes you need to

Deconstruct
Decay
Dissolve

Before you can become
Evolved

Darling,

If you're feeling confused,

Read some philosophy books

They will validate your
current state
of bewilderment
Rendering you no longer
confused
about whether you should be
confused

Darling,

Even the moon
Knows when to
Wax and Wane
Be full and new
Start fresh, Regain

Crescent
Gibbous
Ephemeral

Like the Moon
You are Processual
Again & Again
Eclipse & Remain

Darling,

I know you love lists
So do I!

But life is not a
Checkbox Enterprise

It's more like the immortal jellyfish

Just when we get to a certain point
We revert, regress
Start over,
Begin again
Anew

Darling,

Your lips
were made
for
juicy pears

Darling,

Your hugs could
        heal a thousand souls
Your kisses
        mend a million holes
Your soothing words
        Inspire semiological rolls.
Yet you hide
        Behind
        Inside
A Cluster of Doubt
        Shell of Insecurity
        Web of Precarious Drought
Ill-defined
        Imposter
        Fraud
Forgetting your mission
        Succumbing to some sort of
        syndrome

Darling,

Engorged are the breasts
From which sweet honey flows

A nectar so divine
only
the most suitable
may drink of your wine

Darling,

Your Gift, Your Light, Your Love
Your most precious gems
You too freely give
Before you allow them to
deem themselves worthy

They take advantage
They run off with your
precious stones
Leaving you empty, broken,
And all alone!

Lock up your most prized pieces
Save that key
And show only those
Who, with high regard, will
Utmost Revere Your Bequeathing

Darling,

You are never alone

If that feeling arises
…
Check first to see if
It is you who has abandoned you

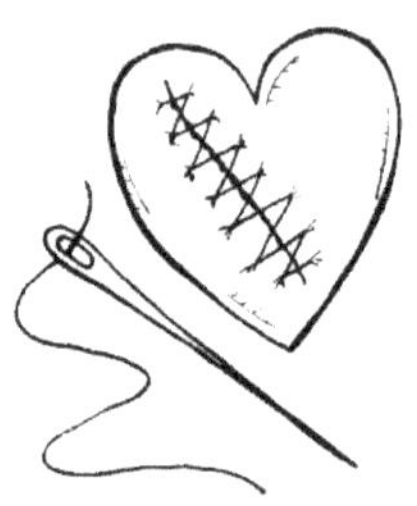

Darling,

Thinks + Overthinks =
No Sleeps

Unattached Thinks
+
Noticed Life Winks
=
More Sleeps

Darling,

Abundance Flows

Unless you build a dam

Then honey,
That's on you

Darling,

Seek inside
For
What it is
You wish to find

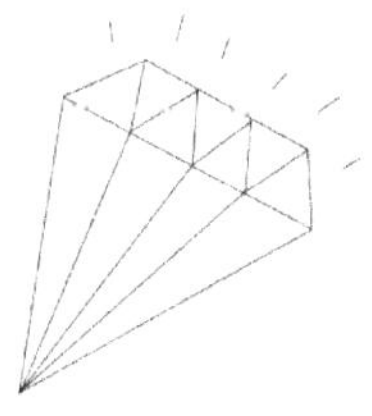

Darling,

My deepest gratitude!

Wishing that
you love
&
Celebrate you

Each and every day!

Find Me:

Instagram: @soulful.susie

@snapturethemoment

TikTok: SoulfulSusie

Twitter: SoulfulSusie

YouTube: Soulful Susie

Amazon: amazon.com/author/susiemolek

Pixabay Line Art Images:

Lotus, Mug, Relax: by OpenClipart-Vectors

Rose with LOVE stem, Think, Woman, Bee

       Images by Bianca Van Dijk

3 Tulips by zazufiane

Heart Finger Print, Octopus, Bird

       Images by Gordon Johnson

Tear by Clker-Free-Vector-Images

Leaf Plant by Yandi ▢ yandidesigns.com

Cake by Piotr Sanocki

Curves by David Zydd from

Pear by OneCoffeGuy

Mend Heart by Vic_B

Diamond by StL20

Mermaid Dolphin by DG-RA, Rafael Javier

* 9 7 9 8 8 4 3 0 6 7 8 1 6 *